REAL REVOLUTIONARIES

THE REAL
JAMES
MADISON
THE TRUTH BEHIND THE LEGEND

by Danielle Smith-Llera

Content Consultant:
Richard Bell
Associate Professor of History
University of Maryland, College Park

COMPASS POINT BOOKS
a capstone imprint

Real Revolutionaries is published by Compass Point Books,
1710 Roe Crest Drive, North Mankato, Minnesota 56003
www.capstonepub.com

**Library of Congress Cataloging-in-Publication data is available on the Library of Congress
website.**
Names: Smith-Llera, Danielle, 1971– author.
Title: The real James Madison : the truth behind the legend / Danielle Smith-Llera.
Description: North Mankato, Minnesota : Capstone Press, 2019. | Series: Real Revolutionaries |
"Compass Point Books." | Includes bibliographical references and index.
Identifiers: LCCN 2019014880 (print) | LCCN 2019015962 (ebook) | ISBN 9780756562564
(eBook PDF) | ISBN 9780756562526 (library binding)
Subjects: LCSH: Madison, James, 1751–1836—Juvenile literature. | Presidents—United States—
Biography—Juvenile literature.
Classification: LCC E342 (ebook) | LCC E342 .S563 2019 (print) | DDC 973.5/1092 [B]—dc23
LC record available at https://lccn.loc.gov/2019014880

Editorial Credits
Mandy Robbins, editor; Sarah Bennett, designer; Eric Gohl, media researcher; Kathy McColley,
production specialist

Photo Credits
Alamy: age footstock, 50, GL Archive, 40–41, History and Art Collection, 23, Niday
Picture Library, 55, PAINTING, cover, 1; Getty Images: Library of Congress, 49, Universal
History Archive, 44; Granger: 29; Library of Congress: 13; National Archives and Records
Administration: 11; North Wind Picture Archives: 18–19, 20, 33, 35, 38; Wikimedia: Billy
Hathorn, 57, Princeton University Art Museum, 6, Public Domain, 9, 15 (all), 27, 31

Design Elements
Shutterstock

All internet sites appearing in back matter were available and accurate when this book was sent to
press.

Printed and bound in the USA
PA49

Contents

CHAPTER ONE
SERVING A NEW NATION

Cannon, muskets, and rifles helped American colonists win freedom from Great Britain. But a young Virginia lawmaker named James Madison was far from the battles of the Revolutionary War (1775–1783). He was sharpening tools that would help shape the new nation—words, pen, and paper. Best remembered as "the Father of the Constitution," James Madison helped write the guide for a new type of government. His Bill of Rights outlined freedoms the government could never take away from its people. He served in the government as a member of Congress, secretary of state, and president. Historic documents in Madison's easy-to-read handwriting remind Americans of the ideals that built the nation.

FATHER OF THE CONSTITUTION

Madison did not want to miss a single minute of the 1787 Constitutional Convention. The 36-year-old delegate from Virginia arrived in Philadelphia 11 days early. Delegates from all 13 states were meeting there to review the 10-year-old plan of government called the Articles of Confederation. Under it, the president served as the head of Congress and did not have the power that presidents do today. Congress decided how to solve problems between the states and with foreign countries. The Articles also gave states freedoms they never enjoyed as colonies under the British king, such as raising their own official, organized state armies.

Madison believed state governments were too powerful and the federal government was too weak under the Articles. They did not even allow the federal government to handle a recent violent revolt in Massachusetts. Madison had a plan to make the young nation stable and strong. He believed it needed a brand-new constitution. It would give the federal government more power. Other delegates agreed with him. They were called Federalists.

But many of the 55 state delegates in Philadelphia disapproved of Madison's plan. The new nation had just broken free of Great Britain. A strong federal government seemed like another monarchy, the enemy of democracy. What's more, Madison's voice was soft and speaking to large groups felt awkward. How could he possibly persuade them of the merits of his plan?

Hardworking Madison arrived in Philadelphia well-prepared for the battle ahead. He had served in Virginia's state government. The studious young man had also spent the winter reading at his Virginia plantation, Montpelier. He took notes about history and previous governments. As Madison saw it, government had to be powerful enough to control its people. Yet it also had to be kept from becoming too powerful.

Madison may have been soft-spoken, but he arrived at the convention with clear ideas and a written plan. His "Virginia Plan" described a federal government with new powers. These included forcing states to pay federal taxes and obey federal laws. Yet Madison's plan called for a complex government structure to limit its powers. Three groups would share decision-making: the legislative, executive, and judicial branches. Even Congress would be divided into two lawmaking bodies. Madison and other

Howard Chandler Christy painted *Scene at the Signing of the Constitution of the United States* in 1940, 153 years after the event.

Federalists convinced other delegates that this system of checks and balances would force the government to act fairly.

But many questions remained. Behind windows shut for secrecy, delegates debated for nearly four months. How much power would the president have? How would Congress represent large and small states fairly? A majority of delegates finally decided on an acceptable form of the U.S. Constitution on September 17, 1787. Now, for the new government to be approved, at least nine of the 13 states had to support it.

Madison took up his pen to help convince state legislatures to ratify the Constitution. For months, essays appeared in newspapers written by three anonymous writers. What the public didn't know is that they were actually written by Madison and his fellow delegates Alexander Hamilton and John Jay. These articles were called the *Federalist Papers*. They explained how the federal government would work under the new Constitution. They assured readers that it would have few powers compared to state governments.

Madison also left his writing desk to nudge lawmakers in his home state to vote for the Constitution. During debates at the Virginia Ratification Convention, Madison faced Patrick Henry, one of the Constitution's fiercest opponents. Henry was an outspoken anti-Federalist. Madison met Henry's dramatic debate style with calmness, logic, and assurances that the new government would not be able to grow dangerously powerful.

Madison's calm logic didn't entirely convince the group. In order to win over Virginia's delegates, Madison had to make a promise. Henry and others believed that the Constitution was missing a crucial part. They wanted a list of freedoms that no federal or state government could ever take away. Madison promised that he would write the document once the Constitution was ratified. When the new government met in September 1789, Madison presented the Bill of Rights. It described freedoms people in the U.S. still enjoy today, such as freedom of speech.

The manuscript of the Constitution of the United States is now held in the National Archives Building in Washington, D.C.

CHAMPION OF THE FIRST PRESIDENT

Even before he became president, Madison influenced the executive branch. Many Americans worried that a president would rule like a monarch. Madison hoped the nation's first president could reassure Americans that the new government was fair. Madison believed that the best person for the job was George Washington.

Without Madison, Washington may never have been president. Madison helped convince the reluctant Revolutionary War hero to come to the 1787 Constitutional Convention. There Washington was unanimously elected to lead the convention. Madison stayed close, sitting across from him. After the convention, Madison kept Washington updated on the Virginia Ratification Convention through weekly letters from Richmond.

Madison even wrote George Washington's first public words as president. Washington delivered his inaugural address to Congress on April 30, 1789. Madison had rewritten Washington's 70-page first draft into this 10-minute speech. Its message reflected Madison's beliefs. It reminded Americans that the president could not rule like a monarch. The Constitution gave Congress great power over the government. Congress could even amend the Constitution.

Madison continued to influence the presidency, even as a member of Congress. Madison wrote the House of Representatives' official messages to the president.

President George Washington delivered his inaugural address on April 30, 1789.

Instead of writing his official response, Washington trusted Madison to do it. Madison's pen helped the legislative and executive branches function during these early years of the nation. But Madison faced competition for influence over the president's ideas and actions.

Washington also depended on another advisor with a persuasive pen—Alexander Hamilton. Hamilton was a member of Washington's Cabinet. Madison and his former *Federalist Papers* coauthor soon clashed over political ideas. And Washington usually agreed with Hamilton. For example, Washington agreed with Hamilton's plan to set up a national bank to control the states' debts. Madison believed this bank was not allowed by the Constitution.

Eventually, trouble with Great Britain proved that Madison had lost influence over the president. Madison believed the U.S. had to deal firmly with British ships harassing U.S. ships. But Washington and Hamilton wanted to keep peace with the former colonial power. Washington approved a treaty in 1794 that favored Great Britain. It outraged Madison and many others. Madison requested details about this treaty from Washington. But Washington told Madison that he was overstepping his power as a member of the House of Representatives. The Constitution only allowed the Senate to advise the president on treaties and foreign relations.

Though he had lost some influence, Madison's ideas still echoed through Washington's last public words—alongside Hamilton's. Washington's "Farewell Address" was published in newspapers in 1796. While Hamilton edited it, Madison's words were the foundation. Washington's first draft borrowed from an unused speech Madison had written for him years earlier. Despite their differences, Madison, Washington, and Hamilton helped make history together.

NEW PARTY FOUNDER

From the beginning, the young nation was divided by clashing opinions about government. But Madison believed that this disagreement was acceptable. After all, the Bill of Rights protected the freedom of speech.

Madison himself helped Americans organize a new political party. It opposed the ideas of the Federalist Party.

Madison and Hamilton were once on the same side. They shared so many ideas that they pretended the *Federalist Papers* were written by one person. However, four years later, they used their pens as weapons against each other. People read their clashing ideas in newspapers in what was then the nation's capital—Philadelphia.

Alexander Hamilton

Madison and others worried that the federal government was mostly helping a small group of wealthy, powerful people. They blamed Federalists who supported the national bank. Opponents of federalism also believed Washington's government supported northern merchants and factory owners. They believed the needs of southern farmers were neglected.

Madison had a powerful friend, a fellow Virginia plantation owner, who shared his frustration. Thomas Jefferson was Washington's secretary of state. Jefferson also disagreed with the influence of Hamilton's ideas on

Thomas Jefferson

the president—and on the *Gazette of the United States*. This Philadelphia newspaper published articles that firmly supported Washington's Federalist government. So in 1791, Jefferson started a new Philadelphia paper, the *National Gazette*. Madison was one of its first writers. Madison's pen took aim at Federalist ideas. He criticized Federalists for following the Constitution too loosely. He also criticized Federalists for not giving people enough freedom.

In a 1792 newspaper article, Madison named these opponents of federalism the "Republican Party." It would come to be called the Democratic-Republican Party. Beginning in 1793, Democratic-Republican clubs formed in small towns and cities across the nation. They criticized Federalists for trusting wealthy, educated people to govern. They believed working-class people should have a voice in government too. For this reason, they admired the French Revolution, a fight against monarchy. But for Federalists, the French Revolution was proof that a government must keep order with a firm hand. Federalists admired Great Britain's stable government, which was controlled by a monarch. Both parties viciously argued and insulted each other during debates and in newspapers.

The development of two political parties sparked the beginning of an American tradition—the political compromise. Madison was one of the first politicians to realize the value of compromise. Madison said that the Constitution was written because opponents gave up

something to move forward. Madison made a compromise
when he voted to support Hamilton's national bank.
In exchange for Madison's vote, Hamilton supported
moving the nation's capital closer to the south. Madison's
gift for compromise would serve the nation for decades.

SECRETARY OF STATE

For more than eight years, Madison dedicated himself to
the legislative branch. He wrote laws, debated, and voted
as a member of Congress. But in 1801, his career took
a major turn. He moved over to the executive branch.
Thomas Jefferson was newly elected as the third U.S.
president. He selected Madison as secretary of state. The
secretary of state makes important decisions about dealing
with other nations. Jefferson trusted his friend Madison.
They shared the same Democratic-Republican ideals.

Stressful and difficult decisions lay ahead for Madison,
particularly in relations with France and Great Britain.
In 1801, France's aggressive military leader, Napoleon
Bonaparte, took over a vast area west of the United States.
It was called the Louisiana Territory. The Mississippi
River ran through it and emptied into the ocean at
New Orleans. Madison believed that this wide river
was the best waterway for profitable American cargo to
reach worldwide ports. Some Americans called for an
army to take New Orleans by force. The French seemed
ready to send soldiers there too.

Madison and Jefferson were certain money could solve this problem. War with Great Britain had left France hungry for cash. Napoleon offered to sell the Louisiana Territory to the United States. But a concern held Jefferson back. Did the Constitution permit the federal government to buy land to expand its borders? Madison assured him that the Louisiana Purchase of 1803 did not violate any part of the Constitution. Madison's assurance convinced Jefferson to make the deal. It resulted in the United States doubling in size!

Madison also hoped to solve troubles with Great Britain without violence. That would prove terribly difficult. Since Washington's presidency, British ships harassed U.S. ships trading with Europe. They seized cargo ships and even captured sailors to force into the British Navy. When Great Britain and France went to war in 1804, the British navy grew even more aggressive. A British ship made a bold attack just off the coast of Virginia in June 1807. It attacked a U.S. ship, the *Chesapeake*, killing three sailors and wounding

18 more. The British kidnapped several survivors they claimed had deserted the British Navy. Many outraged Americans and government leaders now called for war.

U.S. forces were no match for the powerful British navy. Madison persuaded Jefferson to strike back nonviolently. He suggested halting trade. To that end, Congress passed the Embargo of 1807. The results were not what Madison had hoped for. Many Americans in northern cities reacted in anger. They depended on busy

The British Navy often captured American sailors that they claimed had deserted British forces.

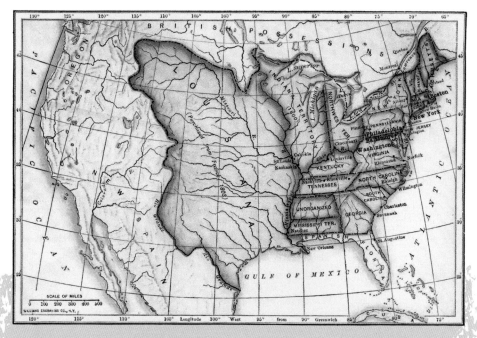

The United States doubled in size as a result of the Louisiana Purchase.

ports to provide jobs and profits. Now their ships were forbidden to sail. Warehouses filled up with waiting cargo. Southern farmers watched crop prices drop with dismay. Opponents called the embargo a sickness infecting every corner of the nation. Meanwhile, Great Britain did not suffer. It received illegal shipments from American merchants or turned to other countries for necessities.

Congress loosened the unpopular embargo in 1809, the year Madison was elected president. But the problems with Great Britain did not disappear. In fact, the war Madison had tried to avoid would break out during his own presidency.

FOURTH PRESIDENT

On March 4, 1809, Madison was inaugurated as the fourth U.S. president. Looking nervous in a black suit, Madison delivered his speech. In a businesslike way, he laid out the options then facing the nation. The U.S. could either accept Great Britain's unfair treatment or go to war.

Madison knew that many Americans were ready to go to war. The British were harassing Americans on land too. They encouraged American Indian allies to antagonize the Americans who had moved in on native land along the nation's western border. What's more, the attack on the *Chesapeake* had united much of the United States in hatred of Great Britain. French warships had helped Americans win that war against Great Britain. But France was no ally now. The pro-British attitudes of Federalist leaders had soured that helpful alliance.

Madison puzzled over what to do. The embargo had backfired. Negotiating a fair trade agreement with either Great Britain or France had failed too. His popularity was sinking. He also worried about the new challenge of commanding a war. On the other hand, it seemed like a good time to strike. Great Britain was already busy fighting Napoleon in Europe.

Madison knew a war would create many new problems for the nation. But he gave in to the wishes of members of his own political party. He asked Congress to consider declaring war. Congress members debated fiercely.

Federalists had always supported Great Britain, but Democratic-Republicans outnumbered them. In June 1812, Congress voted to declare war on Great Britain. Madison was re-elected for a second term shortly after the War of 1812 had begun.

Madison planned to attack British-held Canada. Snatching territory could force Great Britain to negotiate a peace treaty quickly. But the war lasted three long years. British soldiers and their American Indian allies pushed back U.S. attempts to invade Canada. Meanwhile, British ships choked off U.S. trade with a blockade along the East Coast. Worse still for the American cause, the British defeated Napoleon in 1814. They turned their full attention to war with the U.S. They brought the fighting right to Madison's doorstep.

On August 24, 1814, British soldiers battled past U.S. forces and charged into the nation's capital with torches. They left the Capitol Building and the White House in flames. Madison had rushed to join the battle, armed with two borrowed pistols. He was nearly captured by the British before fleeing the city along with his soldiers. Madison would never live in the White House again.

The British expected this humiliation would force the United States to give up. Instead, the burning of Washington, D.C., inflamed the anger of the nation. A battle just one month later gave Americans hope for victory. U.S. battleships defeated the British in a fight for Baltimore. American Francis Scott Key wrote the patriotic poem "Star-Spangled Banner" during the battle in which the British siege ended in failure.

The U.S. and Great Britain signed the Treaty of Ghent in December 1814. It was a truce. The countries agreed to return all conquered territory. The British promised to stop capturing U.S. sailors for its navy. They no longer needed to since the war with France was over.

For Americans, the War of 1812 was a second war for independence from British power. Madison was swept up in a wave of new popularity. While presenting the peace treaty to Congress, Madison spoke with optimism about the nation's future and of "happiness & harmony, in every section of our beloved Country."

In 1914, Amédée Forestier painted *The Signing of the Treaty of Ghent, Christmas Eve, 1814* to celebrate 100 years of peace between Great Britain and the United States.

CHAPTER TWO
A MAN OF CONTRADICTIONS

*M*adison has always been a puzzle, even to the people of his time. Though a public figure, he was often private about his thoughts. Often he was misunderstood. A few friends and colleagues knew the struggles behind Madison's legendary accomplishments.

BILL OF RIGHTS SUPPORTER?

Madison fulfilled the promise he made at the Virginia Ratification Convention. He rose to stand before fellow Congress members on June 8, 1789. It was the first session of Congress under the new Constitution. He proposed the Bill of Rights. Madison explained to Congress that making changes, or amendments, to the Constitution would win over anyone who doubted the document's fairness.

Given his proposal of the Bill of Rights, it would seem fair to assume he was a big supporter of it. But that wouldn't be true. At first, Madison was disgusted by the idea of the Bill of Rights. It seemed unnecessary. He believed the Constitution already contained all the protections people needed. He even thought that a bill of rights could be dangerous. If a right was not included, could it then be denied by the government? Hamilton, Madison's ally at the time, agreed.

But Madison's ideas began to shift soon after the Virginia Ratification Convention. His letters to Jefferson show his strict Federalist attitude toward the Constitution beginning to relax. Madison was realistic about human nature too. "Wherever there is an interest and power to do wrong," Madison said, "wrong will generally be done." So Madison grew to accept that people needed protection from the government.

As with writing the Constitution, Madison took into account the opinions of many people. He collected 200 amendments suggested by state governments. Using his skill at simplifying ideas, he wrote up a short list. They included the right to free speech and the right to a fair trial if suspected of a crime. Madison had to make a compromise for the Bill of Rights to be approved by Congress. He gave up on an amendment to protect citizens against unconstitutional state laws. Congress passed just 10 amendments. They were ratified by the states in 1791.

The Bill of Rights was a triumph for Madison. The list of amendments to the Constitution continues to grow and now totals 27. Aside from protecting the rights of U.S. citizens, they also make the job of judges in the courtroom easier. The judicial branch makes sure laws do not violate the Constitution. The Bill of Rights helps define the laws of the nation more clearly. "If you're looking for Madison's monument, look around," Chief Supreme Court Justice John G. Roberts said in 2008. "Look around at a free country governed by the rule of law."

JEFFERSON'S PUPPET OR PARTNER?

Federalists were certain their candidates would win the 1809 presidential election. After the hugely unpopular embargo, how could Secretary of State Madison have a chance at the presidency? Madison's own political party seemed out to get him too. They accused him of being a power-hungry Federalist in disguise. Jefferson worked hard to support his longtime friend and colleague. He convinced fellow Democratic-Republicans not to join the Federalists against Madison. Jefferson's persuasion was successful, and Madison won the presidency.

But did the low-key Madison always depend on the charismatic Jefferson for his successes? Madison always seemed to be following in Jefferson's footsteps, from serving in the Virginia government to secretary of state to president. Many politicians of the time saw Madison as

The Bill of Rights refers to the first 10 amendments to the U.S. Constitution.

Jefferson's sidekick or puppet. But the two men considered each other equals, even if others did not. Madison joined the Virginia Council of State in 1779 when Jefferson was governor. They shared power the way the president and Congress do. The men worked together every day. Their respect for and friendship with each other grew.

The men also combined different skills to form a productive partnership. Jefferson's strength was persuasive writing and speaking. Meanwhile, Madison's logical mind helped him explain complicated political ideas in ways that seemed simple.

For example, together they helped make freedom of religion a state law and a federal law. In 1773, Madison learned colonists were jailed near his plantation for practicing religions not permitted by England. Jefferson wrote a bill giving all Virginians freedom of religion in 1786. Madison adjusted the bill's language, wrote arguments to support it, and collected signatures from many Virginia supporters. It survived the vote in the Virginia legislature. A few years later, Madison added freedom of religion to his Bill of Rights.

Without Madison's help, Jefferson might have given up his political career. Difficulties struck Jefferson in the early 1780s. During the Revolutionary War, lawmakers accused him of abandoning Virginia's government by fleeing during a British invasion. The next year, he mourned the death of his wife. Jefferson retreated to his plantation. Then Madison offered him a job he could not refuse.

He had nominated Jefferson to help negotiate a treaty with Great Britain. Thanks to his friend, Jefferson left his plantation to rejoin lawmakers in guiding the nation.

Jefferson encouraged Madison's career too. He sent trunks full of books on government and history from Paris, France, to Madison's home of Montpelier in Virginia. These books helped Madison develop the ideas he brought to the 1787 Constitutional Convention. Madison later took care of Jefferson's books too. As president, Madison approved the purchase of Jefferson's private library for the Library of Congress.

Madison asked Jefferson to send him the books listed here from Paris.

When Jefferson died, he left his gold-topped walking stick to Madison. They had been friends for 50 years. Madison worked to protect his friend's memory. He shared details of Jefferson's life with biographers. He also defended Jefferson's views when political groups twisted his ideas to support their causes.

MILITARY HERO OR ZERO?

Torches burned in the streets of Washington in early February 1815. But this time, they weren't in the hands of invading British soldiers. These fires lit streets full of crowds celebrating U.S. victory. To protect New Orleans, poorly equipped U.S. soldiers (with the help of French pirates) had built dirt walls to box in British soldiers. After more than two weeks of facing U.S. fire, the British sailed away. Today Madison is remembered as the victorious commander-in-chief of the War of 1812.

But does Madison deserve credit for this U.S. victory? As president, Madison served as the nation's highest military leader. He attached decorative ribbons to his hat to mark his new role as leader of a country at war. But Madison's only military experience was helping to organize local fighters in the first year of the Revolutionary War. He often suffered from poor health and never saw battle during the revolution.

Nearly 40 years later, Madison was the first president to manage a war. He often left major decisions up to his

military leaders. But that didn't always serve him well.
Madison's military leaders fumbled his plan to invade
Canada. General William Hull promised him a quick
invasion. But once in position at a fort in present-day
Michigan, Hull lost his nerve. He surrendered the fort
before a single shot was fired. In what is now Ontario, a
British army of just 1,000 soldiers defeated U.S. General
James Wilkinson's 4,000 men. In another attack in
Ontario, Colonel Winfield Scott captured a British fort.
But the British recaptured it. Then they captured the U.S.
fort to win full control of the Niagara River.

However, some of Madison's military leaders did win
U.S. victories. One took place on Lake Erie. The British
destroyed U.S. naval commander Oliver Hazard Perry's
ship. He switched ships and led the U.S. navy to victory.

Commander Perry led a life boat that rowed to U.S. victory
in the Battle of Lake Erie.

Many blamed the war's early failures on Madison's secretary of war, John Armstrong. Some blamed Madison even more. "Our President has not those commanding talents, which are necessary to control those about him," said Democratic-Republican Congress member John Calhoun. Armstrong imagined the British would invade Baltimore, not Washington, even as 4,500 British soldiers landed east of the capital. From there, rivers carried them to Washington. Madison believed Armstrong until news arrived that the British were close. Then Madison dashed off on horseback. He joined the poorly armed band of locals called to defend the capital. The president rode too far, nearly running unprotected into the advancing British. Luckily, a violent storm drove the British out of the capital. Rain put out the fires they had set.

Today, many historians admire Madison's leadership despite his mistakes. Madison was a determined commander-in-chief. He did not give up after terrible losses. Shortly after the burning of Washington, U.S. soldiers defeated British troops near the border with Canada. Three days later, U.S. forces resisted British forces in Baltimore. Even John Adams, the second U.S. president and a Federalist, said that Madison "acquired more glory, and established more Union than all three of his predecessors."

President Madison (in gray) discusses a plan of action with his generals during the War of 1812.

ONLY POPULAR BECAUSE OF HIS WIFE?

Madison did not often impress people in person, especially when compared with other statesmen. Washington or Jefferson were at least 6 feet (183 centimeters) tall, while Madison's height was about 5 foot, 4 inches (163 cm) tall. Looking weak and frail did not help the impression he made. When 30-year-old Madison first arrived in Congress, one delegate thought he was a college student. Others were insulting. "No bigger than half a piece of soap," is how one person described him. Enemies disrespectfully called him "Little Jemmy." British soldiers ransacking the White House called him "the little president."

Madison was awkward and serious. His quiet voice was easily drowned by a crowd's murmur as he stiffly read notes tucked inside his hat. Listeners often wished he had more enthusiasm. He clothed himself entirely in black as if "dressed for a funeral," some said. In fact, his approach to fashion was so businesslike that he owned only one suit at a time.

Madison might have been a very unpopular president if not for his wife, Dolley. Her heroism during the burning of Washington captured the admiration of the nation. With the British just miles from the president's house, she grabbed a copy of the Declaration of Independence. She also directed servants to take down the 8-foot (2.4 meter) portrait of George Washington in the dining room. She fled with these precious objects to safety.

Dolley Madison instructed workers to move Gilbert Stuart's portrait of George Washington before fleeing the White House.

Dolley's lively personality also made up for Madison's solemn one. In fact, many consider her his political partner. Her popularity helped connect him with many people important to his political career. Madison enjoyed writing letters to friends and colleagues. But his wife enjoyed visiting people and going to parties. She created a presidential tradition by throwing a grand ball on the night of Madison's first inauguration. And despite her elegant dresses and turbans decorated with pearls, people appreciated that the First Lady was not arrogant.

Yet without Dolley at his side, Madison still won over rooms of delegates at the Constitutional Convention and later, members of Congress. People did find his public speeches boring. But they admired the wisdom of his ideas and the logical way he presented them. People lucky enough to meet Madison in a small group found that he was not all business. He spoke freely and naturally, sprinkling conversations with entertaining stories. It is no surprise that both Jefferson and James Monroe, the fifth president, valued their friendship with Madison and prized his letters.

Despite Madison's less impressive qualities, people's respect for his wisdom has only grown over time. With both affection and respect, people have called him "the great little Madison." And when he died in 1836, a headline read "The Sage of Montpelier is no more!" Today, the official monument to Madison is his library. The James Madison Memorial Building in Washington, D.C., spans about 1.5 million square feet (139,355 square meters).

CHAPTER THREE
MYSTERIOUS MADISON

*M*adison avoided being the center of attention. As a leader, he was undramatic and hard-working. Yet his major accomplishments in shaping and serving in the federal government are well known. He also left his mark on history in lesser-known ways. Madison always worked to protect what was most important to him—the unity of the nation and the rights of its people.

A STEADY HAND IN TURBULENT TIMES

The first Americans to die in the War of 1812 were not shot by the British. An angry mob of fellow Americans was to blame. Just days after Congress declared war, deadly riots broke out in Baltimore. Federalists were enraged to be at war with a country they considered an ally. To Democratic-Republicans, this attitude was unpatriotic and unacceptable. During the riots, pro-war Democratic-Republicans tortured an editor of an anti-war newspaper to death. It looked like Madison had more to handle than fighting the British. He had to keep the U.S. from slipping into a civil war.

The Baltimore riots did not stop Federalists from protesting the war. In Congress, Federalist members had voted unanimously against it. Madison could not even depend on the full support of his own political party. One-quarter of Democratic-Republican members of Congress voted against the war or chose not to vote at all.

Federalists in New England were desperate. They had already spent years suffering under embargoes on trade. Now British warships blocked trade across the ocean. They blamed their troubles on "Mr. Madison's War." They even sent delegates to a convention in Hartford, Connecticut. There they prepared demands of the federal government. They demanded help for their money troubles triggered by trade problems. They demanded their citizens be excused from serving as soldiers in a war they did not support. A few delegates even considered the drastic measure of breaking away, or seceding, from the nation.

Madison's reaction to opposition during the war impresses historians to this day. He openly criticized state governors who did not contribute soldiers. However, he never tried to stop people from criticizing him personally. He stood by the first amendment in the Bill of Rights. It protects the rights of people to express their opinions. It also protects their right to protest peacefully against the government. Newspapers published vicious attacks on his ideas, his actions, and even his physical appearance. But not even calls for his removal as president, or impeachment, could shake his support of the freedom of speech.

A decade earlier, Madison had defended freedom of speech from another president. John Adams was fed up with sharp criticism printed in Democratic-Republican newspapers. He urged Federalist Congress members to pass the Sedition Act of 1798. The law punished anyone who wrote criticism of the government with fines or jail. Madison, a member of the Virginia House of Delegates at the time, was horrified that leaders would not hear any opinions different from their own. He jumped to defend the Bill of Rights and turned to his favorite weapon, his pen. He wrote the "Virginia Resolution," which declared the new federal laws unconstitutional because they violated the Bill of Rights. The resolution was accepted by the Virginia Legislature.

As president, Madison respected the first amendment. He didn't feel the need to silence his critics. His successful leadership during the War of 1812 did that. The peace treaty with Great Britain made them look foolish. In fact, the weakened Federalist Party broke apart about a decade later.

PIRATE FIGHTER

Madison couldn't relax after the end of the War of 1812. U.S. sailors were still in danger of getting kidnapped at sea. It was not Great Britain they feared, but pirates from the Barbary states of North Africa. Pirates from this area made a business of capturing sailors. Their leaders supported these crimes and charged sailors' home countries high fees for their return. These ransoms added up to millions of dollars. Captured sailors were also profitable when sold into slavery. It is possible that North African states captured as many as 1.5 million European and American sailors by 1780.

In 1804, U.S. Commodore Edward Preble's fleet attacked Barbary pirates in the First Barbary War.

Madison believed that the Constitution could protect U.S. sailors at sea. Before the revolution, the British Navy had protected colonial ships from attacks. That protection was gone now. Pirates captured several U.S. ships in 1785. But the newly independent United States was too weak to fight back. Madison offered a solution to the pirate problem. In the *Federalist Papers* he argued that a new, strong government would make the U.S. too powerful to terrorize. He was right. The Constitution gave the new federal government the freedom to build a powerful navy to take on the Barbary pirates.

President Washington had sent negotiators to North Africa in 1795. The U.S. and the Barbary states signed treaties and dozens of captive U.S. sailors were set free. But this peace was costly. The U.S. agreed to pay the Barbary states money, or tribute, to leave their sailors alone in the future. By 1800, 20 percent of the money collected by the U.S. government was used to pay tribute

to Barbary states. Then government leaders in Tripoli demanded more and declared war on the U.S. in 1801. Instead of negotiators, President Jefferson responded with naval ships. The U.S. defeated Tripoli in the First Barbary War in 1805.

President Madison faced the same demand for more tribute money as the presidents before him. But this time it was from Algiers, the largest and most powerful of the Barbary states. Algiers declared war on the United States in 1812 and captured a U.S. ship. The Algerians were bold because Madison could do nothing to stop them. The War of 1812 had just started, and Great Britain was a far greater threat to the U.S.

By 1815, Madison was ready to deal with the pirates. The British blockade was no longer an obstacle to free trade, but Barbary pirates still were. Just one month after the end of the War of 1812, Madison urged Congress to declare war on Algiers. After three years of war with Great Britain, the U.S. navy had grown large and experienced. Armed U.S. ships arrived in the Algerian port and blasted its fleet to splinters. In this brief Second Barbary War, Algiers gave in to U.S. demands. They released captives and promised no future attacks. Algerian pirates would continue to menace sailors at sea. But the U.S. Navy had demonstrated its might to the world. Madison reinforced that idea when he said, "The United States, while they wish for war with no nation, will buy peace with none."

PROTECTOR OF INVENTIONS

Farming is hard work. It has inspired people to develop new technology to make the work easier, faster, and more profitable. Jefferson invented a new kind of plow that pushed through soil with less effort. Washington invented a 16-sided barn to separate wheat grains with horse power. Madison was not an inventor, but he believed that new ideas of all kinds pushed the nation to be more productive and create wealth.

Madison knew the Constitution had to encourage inventors. On August 18, 1787, he made a formal proposal to the delegates at the Constitutional Convention. He suggested that ideas should be protected, like any other property. They should not be borrowed without permission. Madison wanted the federal government to protect inventions with patents. These documents give inventors sole permission to make and sell their inventions.

But some delegates worried that patents were not democratic. If inventors owned their ideas, how could they be useful to anyone else? Madison believed that it was logical for inventors to own their ideas, just as farmers own the crops grown in their fields. He even thought patents inspired inventors to work harder without the fear that others could steal their ideas and make money. Because patents were good for inventors, patents were good for the nation. Madison was persuasive. But as usual, he had to make a compromise to have his idea accepted.

It combined both views on patents. Inventors were allowed to own the rights to their invention, but only for a limited time. The delegates voted unanimously for Madison's proposal.

By 1790, Congress had passed the Patent Act. For the first time in history, inventors did not depend on a monarch to grant a patent. In the U.S., it was now a right. Inventors could claim a patent if their ideas were original. A three-person committee reviewed designs on paper and models for inventions. Jefferson was on this committee.

Eli Whitney invented the cotton gin in 1793.

The public's interest in applying for patents was beyond what Jefferson ever expected. In fact, reviewing the flood of applications for patents took more time than his work as secretary of state. A full-time clerk was put in charge of applications, but the paperwork still piled up.

Congress refused to set up a Patent Office in its own federal building. In 1802, when Madison was secretary of state, he engaged architect and inventor William Thornton to design and oversee a new building to house the Patent Office. During the burning of Washington, D.C., in 1814, Thornton convinced British generals to keep their torches away from the Patent Office. He argued that the hundreds of inventors' models it contained could benefit the whole world.

CHAPTER FOUR
UNFORTUNATE TRUTHS

*I*nside federal and state government buildings, Madison fought for balance. He believed a government needed to be strong enough to protect people's freedoms. Yet it could not be so strong that it took freedoms away. But Madison's life outside this work was messy, complicated, and even heartbreaking. He struggled for balance between his ideals and his life as an owner of enslaved people. He also had overwhelming family troubles that he never did overcome.

RIGHTS DENIED

At 18 years old, Madison left Montpelier to attend Princeton University in 1769. He traveled to New Jersey with a companion named Sawney. Sawney had looked after Madison as a child. But he was not an older brother or uncle. He was an enslaved person, like hundreds of thousands of black people in the United States at that time.

Madison knew it was wrong to treat human beings like property to be bought and sold. But like many plantations in the south, Montpelier depended on the work of more than 100 enslaved people. Like other slaveholders, Madison used twisted logic to justify enslaving people. Madison claimed that slavery protected black people from white people's racism. However, Madison was not just any plantation owner. He was the author of the Bill of Rights. His deeply held ideas about freedom clashed with his lifestyle. Madison's great skill was finding a way to make two conflicting opinions work together. Yet the compromises he made over slavery troubled him his entire life.

He was not the only slaveholder at the Constitutional Convention. He and other delegates did not even want the Constitution to mention slavery. Madison admitted in private letters that he wished slavery was not necessary to plantation life. He even called slavery "unnatural" in the *Federalist Papers*. He wrote of hope that slavery would be abolished one day. Shortly after writing the Bill of Rights, Madison imagined a plan. He wanted to free enslaved people and resettle them in Africa. He also suggested that the U.S. sell western lands to raise the hundreds of millions of dollars to buy their freedom. Yet Madison never freed Sawney or any other enslaved people. He even brought them to serve his family in the White House.

To reach political goals, Madison could push aside his private concerns about slavery. In 1783, he even stated that enslaved people were not fully human. Congress asked each state to contribute money to the federal government. The amount was based on its population. Southern states did not want their enslaved people counted. Northerners wanted southerners to pay more and insisted enslaved people be counted fully. Madison offered a cold-hearted compromise. He proposed that each enslaved person should count as three-fifths of a person. His suggestion did not get enough votes in Congress. But Madison's dehumanizing suggestion was not forgotten. Four years later, delegates at the Constitutional Convention debated how many representatives each state could send to Congress. Southerners now wanted enslaved people counted fully so they could have more representatives. But northerners disagreed. This time delegates agreed on Madison's suggestion and the "three-fifths compromise" was adopted.

Madison also supported the slave trade so that the Constitution could pass. Many slaveholders, including Madison, believed that shipping people to sell between foreign countries was unacceptable. To them, keeping people enslaved on plantations was less brutal. But Madison pushed this belief aside. Three states threatened to reject the Constitution if the government banned the slave trade. To get their votes, Madison supported the slave trade for 20 more years.

Madison never put his ideas about slavery into action. He did not even free the people enslaved at Montpelier after his death, as Washington did. Almost 30 years after Madison's death, the 13th amendment of the Constitution finally made slavery illegal.

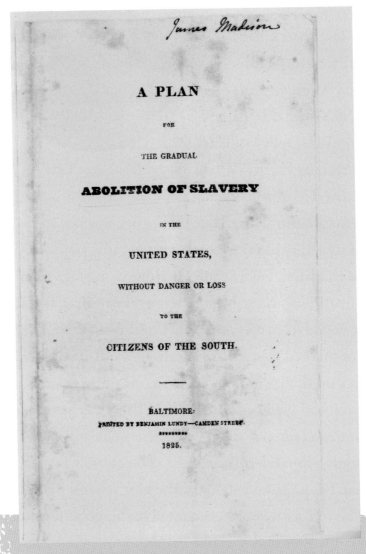

Madison published *A Plan for the Gradual Abolition of Slavery* in 1825.

FAMILY TROUBLE

Madison and his wife
never had children
together. But Dolley
had a little boy named
John Payne Todd.
Yellow fever had killed
Dolley's first husband
and baby William, but
John Payne, her eldest son,
had survived. Dolley called
him "Precious Payne." When
she married Madison, Payne

John Payne Todd

began to call him "Papa." But their story was not so sweet.
People took pity on Madison for having this stepson.

For Madison, Payne proved harder to manage than a
room of arguing delegates or a war against Great Britain.
Those ended in victory, after all. On the other hand,
disaster marked Payne's life. Nothing Madison did was
able to stop that.

Payne had many advantages. Madison was generous
with him and did not claim any of the wealth Payne's
father left behind. Madison set it aside entirely for his
stepson. Payne attended one of the best schools in the
Washington area. People remarked on his good looks and
charm. They treated him like royalty.

Madison and his wife hoped that Payne would also
attend Princeton University, as Madison had. But as

a young man, Payne chose instead to tag along with government leaders on a trip to Europe. Madison thought that travel might mature his stepson, so he sent him on a mission to Russia too. But the young man discovered that he preferred drinking alcohol and gambling to studying. These addictions tormented Payne—and his parents—all his life.

But Madison didn't give up on Payne. He tried many ways to help his stepson stop his dangerous habits. While president, he briefly made Payne his secretary. He put him in charge of his farms. But his stepson did not succeed in any job. Madison even bought him land to plant crops and build a home. Payne named it Toddsberthe. But instead of farming, he dreamed of digging up marble to sell and get rich. That didn't happen.

Payne was an expensive stepson. More than once, he was jailed for being unruly in public. Madison paid to set him free. Payne's gambling and spending were also constant stresses. Madison sold off property and borrowed money to pay his stepson's debts. They totaled about $40,000. That's about $800,000 in today's money. Poor harvests at Montpelier added to Madison's money troubles. After Madison's death, Payne's debts continued to pile up. Dolley had to sell Montpelier.

Payne even damaged Madison's plans for his precious collection of books and writings. Madison wanted his private library to be donated to the University of Virginia after his death. But Payne stole books from it, probably to sell. When Dolley sold Madison's writings to Congress, the collection was incomplete. Payne had raided those too. Over many years, the Library of Congress has slowly undone Payne's damage. Workers have tracked down most of Madison's personal writings. Today the collection totals 12,000 items.

Payne's short and miserable life ended just two and a half years after his mother died. He died of typhoid fever at the age of 59. His gravestone does not hint at his sad story but simply reads: "Beloved Son of Dolley P.T. Madison."

CHAPTER FIVE

MADISON'S GIFTS TO THE NATION

Visitors to Montpelier saw immediately what was most important to Madison. In his entryway, a half-circle window is divided into 13 panes. At that time, the nation was made up of 13 states. In one large room, Madison displayed a portrait of himself, but not as a centerpiece. It was surrounded by busts of Washington, Jefferson, Adams, and other friends and colleagues. After all, he had never claimed to accomplish all that he did by himself. He even resisted being called the "Father of the Constitution." "It ought to be regarded as the work of many heads and many hands," Madison once said.

This modesty has helped make Madison easy to overlook when compared to his famous friends. Madison's writing may not have the flair of Jefferson's.

Madison's leadership style may not have had the appeal of Washington, the revolutionary hero on a white horse. Unlike Washington and Jefferson, Madison's face no longer appears on U.S. money. It had appeared on the $5,000 bill, but that stopped being printed in 1969. However, historians are no longer dismissing him as forgettable. Today some say that he might have been the most important founding father of all.

Madison's shifting opinions have made him seem indecisive. But that flexibility seems to be the key to his success. Later in life, he even came to accept the national bank, the issue that first led him to pull away from Federalists. At the time, Madison did not believe the Constitution gave the federal government the power to create it. But 25 years later, Madison himself approved a second national bank for the nation struggling with war debt. The Constitution had not changed, but Madison's views had. As a young man, Madison followed the Constitution so strictly that even adding a Bill of Rights seemed inappropriate. However, by the time he reached old age, he had learned that following any idea or opinion too strictly or too loosely leads to trouble. A visitor to Montpelier remembered an elderly Madison saying "the Constitution has two enemies—one that would stretch it to death, and one that would squeeze it to death." Madison knew that compromise was the only way to accomplish anything. His 40-year political career proved that.

What never shifted was Madison's dedication to the nation and its changing needs. Even as a 78-year-old, Madison traveled to Richmond for another Constitutional Convention. He was elected a delegate to help rewrite the Virginia Constitution. There Madison spoke in public for the last time, his voice just a whisper. As usual, his audience had to lean in to listen.

Madison does not have a splendid monument in Washington, D.C., like George Washington or Thomas Jefferson. But those who take a closer look at Madison's life and work come to an extraordinary conclusion. "Without Washington, we wouldn't have won the revolution. Without Jefferson, the nation wouldn't have been inspired," said Michael Quinn, president of the Montpelier Foundation. "What made our revolution complete was the genius of Madison. . . . He formed the ideals of the nation."

James Madison is
buried in his family's
cemetery at Montpelier.

MADISON
BORN MARCH 16, 1751
DIED JUNE 28TH 1836

TIMELINE

MARCH 16, 1751
Madison is born in Virginia and grows up at Montpelier
in Orange County.

1769
Madison begins studying at the College of New Jersey, Princeton,
and completes a degree in two years.

APRIL 1776
Madison is elected to the Virginia Convention in Williamsburg,
Virginia, beginning a career in government.

JULY 4, 1776
The Continental Congress approves
the Declaration of Independence.

NOV 17, 1777
Congress adopts the Articles of Confederation during the
Revolutionary War. Madison serves on the Virginia Council
in Williamsburg.

MARCH 1780–DECEMBER 1783
Madison serves as a delegate in the Continental Congress
in Philadelphia.

SEPTEMBER 3, 1783
The Revolutionary War ends.

MAY–SEPTEMBER 1787
Madison serves as the Virginia delegate to the Constitutional
Convention and signs the U.S. Constitution.

1788
The *Federalist Papers* are first published and written
with Alexander Hamilton and John Jay.

MARCH 1788
Madison is elected to the Virginia Ratification Convention, where Patrick Henry argues against the Constitution.

1789-1797
Madison serves in the U.S. House of Representatives.

SEPTEMBER 15, 1794
Madison marries Dolley Payne Todd.

1801-1809
Madison serves as U.S. Secretary of State under President Thomas Jefferson. He helps negotiate the Louisiana Purchase.

1809-1817
Madison serves two terms as the fourth U.S. president.

JUNE 1812-FEBRUARY 1815
The War of 1812 rages.

AUGUST 24-26, 1814
The British burn the White House and Capitol Building in Washington, D.C.

JUNE 28, 1836
Madison dies at home at Montpelier.

GLOSSARY

amend—to change in order to make something more accurate

anonymous—written, done, or given by a person whose name is not known or made public

bill—a written draft of a proposed law

constitution—a set of rules that guides how a country, state, or political organization works

delegate—someone who represents other people at a meeting

embargo—a government ban on trade with foreign countries

executive—the branch of government that carries out the laws of the United States or any state

impeach—to bring formal charges against a public official who may have committed a crime while in office

inauguration—the ceremony of putting a person in office

judicial—the branch of government that has to do with judges interpreting laws in courts

legislative—a branch of government that has the power to make or change laws for a country or state

monarchy—a type of government in which a king or queen is the head of state

ratify—to approve an agreement

siege—a military blockade of a city, to make it surrender

unanimously—when everyone agrees

unconstitutional—not allowed by the constitution of a country, state, or political organization

FURTHER READING

Broadwater, Jeff. *Jefferson, Madison, and the Making of the Constitution*. Chapel Hill, NC: The University of North Carolina Press, 2019.

Krull, Kathleen. *A Kids' Guide to America's Bill of Rights*. New York: HarperCollins, September 15, 2015.

Travis, Cathy. *Constitution Translated for Kids*. Washington, D.C.: CT Bookshelf, 2016.

INTERNET SITES

James Madison Biography
www.biography.com/people/james-madison-9394965

U.S. Constitution
www.brainpop.com/socialstudies/ushistory/usconstitution/

Virtual Tour of Montpelier
www.encyclopediavirginia.org/media_player?mets_filename=evr9571mets.xml

The White House/James Madison
www.whitehouse.gov/about-the-white-house/presidents/james-madison/

SOURCE NOTES

Page 23, "happiness & harmony..." James Madison, "From James Madison to Congress, 18 February 1815," Founders Online, founders.archives.gov/documents/Madison/03-08-02-0523, Accessed March 19, 2019.

Page 25, "Wherever there is..." Myron Magnet, "The Great Little Madison," *City Journal*, Spring 2011, www.city-journal.org/html/great-little-madison-13379.html, Accessed March 19, 2019.

Page 26, "If you're looking for..." Kenneth R. Flether, "Montpelier and the Legacy of James Madison," Smithsonia.com, October 19, 2008, www.smithsonianmag.com/history/montpelier-and-the-legacy-of-james-madison-85354581/, Accessed April 16, 2019.

Page 32, "Our president has not..." "Political Enemies Judge President James Madison Extraordinarily Harshly," National Park Service, www.nps.gov/articles/grading-madison-wartime-president.htm, Accessed March 19, 2019.

Page 32, "acquired more glory..." Ibid., Accessed March 19, 2019.

Page 34, "no bigger than..." "The Great Little Madison," Accessed March 19, 2019.

Page 42, "The United States..." Christopher Hitchens, "Jefferson Versus the Muslim Pirates," *City Journal*, Spring 2007, www.city-journal.org/html/jefferson-versus-muslim-pirates-13013.html, Accessed March 19, 2019.

Page 53, "It ought to be regarded..." "The Second American Revolution," James Madison's Montpelier, www.montpelier.org/learn/the-second-american-revolution, Accessed March 10, 2019.

Page 54, "the Constitution has two enemies..." John E. Semmes. *John H. B. Latrobe and His Times 1803–1891.* Baltimore, MD: The Norman, Remington Co, 1917, p. 245.

Page 56, "Without Washington..." Kenneth R. Fletcher, "Montpelier and the Legacy of James Madison," Smithsonian. com, October 19, 2008, www.smithsonianmag.com/history/ montpelier-and-the-legacy-of-james-madison-85354581/Accessed March 19, 2019.

SELECT BIBLIOGRAPHY

Broadwater, Jeff. *James Madison: A Son of Virginia and a Founder of the Nation*. Chapel Hill: University of North Carolina Press, 2012.

The Great Little Madison
www.city-journal.org/html/great-little-madison-13379.html

How the Louisiana Purchase Changed the World
www.smithsonianmag.com/history/how-the-louisiana-purchase-changed-the-world-79715124/

James Madison
www.whitehouse.gov/about-the-white-house/presidents/james-madison/

The Life of James Madison
www.montpelier.org/learn/the-life-of-james-madison

Noah Feldman. "James Madison's Lessons in Racism." *New York Times*, Oct. 28, 2017. www.nytimes.com/2017/10/28/opinion/sunday/james-madison-racism.html

Semmes, John E. *John H. B. Latrobe and His Times, 1803-1891*. Baltimore, MD: The Norman, Remington Co., 1917.

INDEX